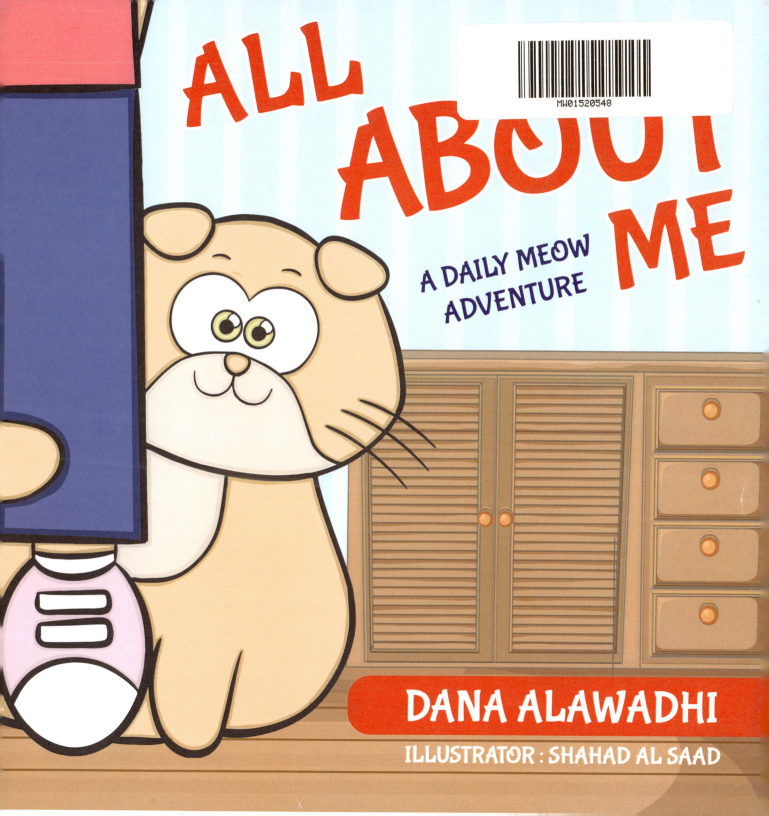

ALL ABOUT ME

A DAILY MEOW ADVENTURE

DANA ALAWADHI

ILLUSTRATOR : SHAHAD AL SAAD

My name is Ginger,
and I love to play,
Especially with my
mommy, May.
With sharp claws,
I fetch the ball,
I'm quick and
nimble, I never fall.

I love to eat chicken and meat,
But my favourite treat is oh so sweet.
Can you guess what it might be?
Turkey, turkey, that's for me!

I lay beside my mommy May,
And sometimes we like to play.
We chase her yarn round and round,
Until we both fall to the ground.

I can sleep on the couch or anywhere,
But my favourite spot is the comfy chair.
If I'm tired, May picks me up,
And she usually gives me a good rub.

If I ever see a little bug,
I make sure to give it a little tug.
Sneaking behind the bug I go,
This is going to be a great show.

My favourite thing to do is lay in the sun,
It's an easy way to have a little fun!
So let's go to the window, my little friend,
Where fun and laughter never end!

I don't like going outside,
But I really love car rides.
So if you see me in a car passing by,
Give me a smile and I'll wave Hi!

Watching the cars
is so much fun,
I imagine touching
them one by one.

I am a very playful cat,
Who has never, ever caught a rat.
I have also tried catching a laser trail,
But it always runs too fast, and I fail!

Do you want to
guess what I did
catch one time?
It was during my
bedtime!
Buzzing here and
there, it was a fly,
I caught it before it
could hit the sky!

Around Nicky, I must be wary,
Her allergy to me is quite scary.
May's sister is dear to me, you know,
But I can't snuggle or give her a show.
I can't give her kisses, but that's okay,
I find other ways to love her every day.

I have a sister just like me,
We look the same, as you can see!
But she has these little hair,
That she thinks isn't fair,
She doesn't like them, but little
does she know,
These little hair of hers can steal the
show!

I'll tell you another,
I also have a twin brother,
Who's always late for supper.
He's always running here and there,
Jumping and playing without a care.

One day, my spider friends and I,
Bob, Barley and Pie, climbed up a tree.
But they left me there, oh, what a fright.
I cried and cried; it didn't feel right.
But then I remembered,
I am brave and strong.

I climbed down the tree; it didn't take long.
I found my way home, all alone.
I shouted out loud, "I did it; I'm proud."

Do you know what zoomies are?
I'll tell you, but it's pretty bizarre!
Zoomies are when cats go silly and fast,
They run, jump, and have a blast!

When I am zooming,
I play hide and seek.
In every little gap,
I'll peek-a-boo sneak!
Behind the curtains or in a
little box,
I'll hide like a clever little fox!

Now that you've met me,
Ginger, your new kitty
friend.
We'll have silly adventures
that seem like they will
never end!
So come on, my friend,
this way we go,
To the door and watch the
little mice show!

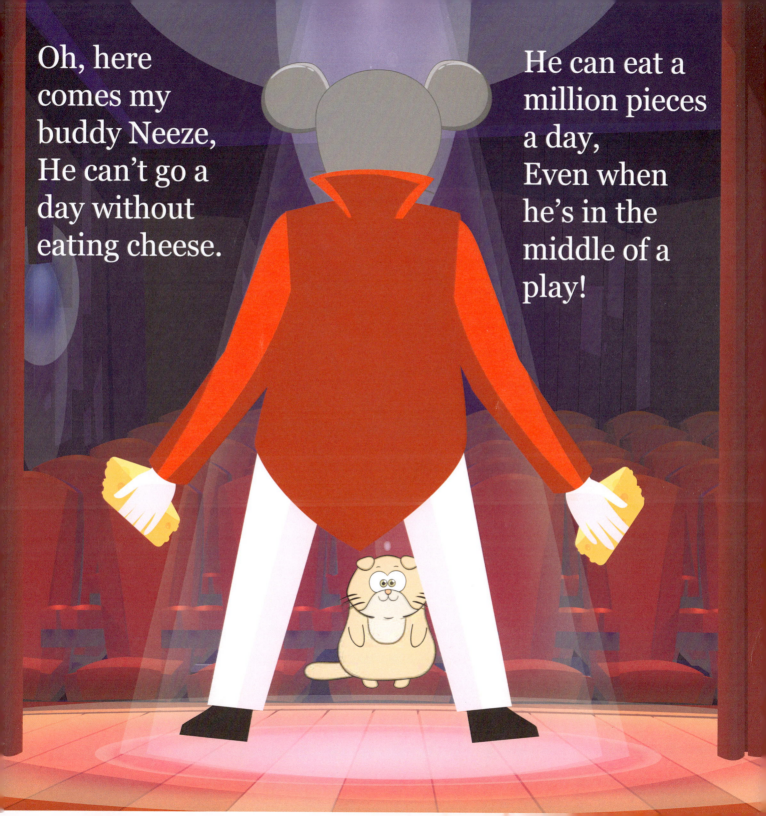

Oh, here comes my buddy Neeze, He can't go a day without eating cheese.

He can eat a million pieces a day, Even when he's in the middle of a play!

Today went by like a bee,
And now, you know all
about me!

Well, now it's time for me to rest,
I'm always active during the night,
at my best.
But now, it's bedtime, and I'll sleep
tight,
Goodnight, my friends. Sleep
well tonight!

Come and join Ginger on an adventure of her life! Ginger will tell you all about her home, siblings, bedtime routine, and, not to forget, her favourite turkeys! Ever since Ginger was a kitten, her love for eating turkey grew!

Meet Dana Alawadhi, a writer and storyteller who is also the president of the Student Council at her school. She loves writing exciting and creative stories for kids. In this story, Dana shares her enormous passion and love for animals, especially her cat, Ginger. When she's not writing, she likes to do gymnastics, cooking, and volleyball. Get ready for thrilling adventures and fun characters in Dana's stories that will keep you hooked.

Printed in the USA
CPSIA information can be obtained
at www.ICGtesting.com
LVRC091940150224
771971LV00007B/130